EISENHOWER

From the War to the White House

Written by Gilles Rahier
In collaboration with Pierre Frankignoulle
Translated by Rebecca Neal

DWIGHT DAVID EISENHOWER   1

Key information
Introduction

BIOGRAPHY   3

Military training
On the ground
Political career

POLITICAL, SOCIAL AND ECONOMIC CONTEXT   8

The postwar period and the start of the Cold War
The containment of Communism and the Red Scare
The 1950s and the Affluent Society
Racial segregation and civil rights
The race for the White House in 1952

HIGHLIGHTS   17

A moderate president
Progressive conservatism
A change in foreign policy
The beginnings of desegregation
The end of McCarthyism
Reelection in 1956 and the Eisenhower Doctrine
Less tense relations with the USSR

IMPACT   28

The Vietnam War
Cuba: a neighbour and an enemy

The Civil Rights Movement during the 1960s

SUMMARY   34

FIND OUT MORE   38

DWIGHT DAVID EISENHOWER

KEY INFORMATION

- **Born:** 14 October 1890 in Denison, Texas.
- **Died:** 28 March 1968 in Washington, D.C.
- **Political party:** the Republican Party.
- **Election dates:**
    - 4 November 1952
    - 6 November 1956.
- **Length of presidency:** eight years.
- **Main achievements:**
    - the end of the Korean War
    - economic recovery and reduced inflation
    - the fight against McCarthyism
    - significant advances in racial desegregation
    - the Eisenhower Doctrine
    - the containment of Communism
    - relative calm in USA-USSR relations.

INTRODUCTION

Dwight David Eisenhower, a hero of the Second World War (1939-1945) and a crucial figure in the liberation of Europe, was nominated as the Republican candidate in the 1952 presidential election. In large part thanks to his image as a great diplomat, he was elected by a comfortable margin over his opponent, the Democrat Adlai Stevenson (1900-1965), who he defeated again in the 1956 election.

He was the first Republican president in 20 years, and formed a moderate government led by the private sector. His presidency also came during a period of many major economic changes, which allowed the country to develop and become what would later be called the Affluent Society. In addition, he had to face the worst domestic troubles that the USA had experienced, such as the paranoia engendered by McCarthyism and the fight against racial segregation.

In the midst of the Cold War (1947-1990), he fought against Communist influence in the world through the doctrine that bears his name. Thanks to his negotiation skills, he managed to somewhat calm the tensions which paralysed relations between the USA and the USSR.

Widely admired across the political spectrum, and later recognised as one of the most popular American presidents, he retired from public life after eight years in office. However, in spite of the warmth he had always displayed, his final speech went down in history because of his warning against the military-industrial complex, which was growing in importance, and the rise of American militarism. In a single stroke, this overturned the view of Eisenhower in the popular imagination.

BIOGRAPHY

Portrait of Dwight D. Eisenhower.

MILITARY TRAINING

Dwight David Eisenhower was born on 14 October 1890, and was the third child of David Jacob Eisenhower (1863-1942) and Ida Elizabeth Stover (1862-1946). The family, which had immigrated from Germany in the 18th century (their surname was originally spelled Eisenhauer), was working-class and deeply religious.

After his relatively mediocre early education in Kansas, Eisenhower entered the United States Military Academy at West Point in 1911. This was where he met Mamie Geneva Doud (1896-1979), the daughter of a successful businessman, who he married in 1916 and with whom he would have two sons. In 1915, he graduated in the middle of his class with the rank of lieutenant.

When the First World War (1914-1918) broke out, Eisenhower asked to be sent to the front, but his request was turned down. Forced to remain in the United States, he served as an instructor in various training centres. Through hard work and perseverance, he managed to climb the ladder of the military hierarchy. In 1924, after serving for two years in the Panama Canal Zone, he continued his military training at Fort Leavenworth in Kansas and the United States Army War College in Pennsylvania. From 1933 to 1939, he served as chief military aide to General Douglas MacArthur (1880-1964) in a region of the Philippines, where he was tasked with overseeing the creation of a local army. On his return to the USA, he was promoted to brigadier general in 1941.

ON THE GROUND

After the attack on the Pearl Harbor naval base by Japanese forces in 1941, the United States entered the Second World War. The time had finally come for Eisenhower to prove himself. He was called on by General George Catlett Marshall (1880-1959) to help draw up plans for the landings in Europe. Placed in charge of the American troops and then the Allied forces in Europe, he decided to launch Operation Torch in North Africa, as well as Operation Husky and Operation Ladbroke in Italy, which would have a lasting impact on the fate of the war, allowing the Allies to create different fronts to divide the enemy troops.

A NEW FRONT TO RELIEVE RUSSIA

In September 1942, the Allied camp had the idea of creating a second military front to relieve the Russian front, where the German war effort was concentrated. They saw this as the only way to win the war. General George Catlett Marshall then tasked Eisenhower with planning a landing in North Africa (namely in Morocco and Algeria, which at that time were French colonies). Helped by the French resistance in the region, they quickly took Algiers and began the Tunisia Campaign (1942-1943).

Shortly afterwards, with the same aim in mind, the high command, led by General Eisenhower, decided on a landing on the coasts of Italy (specifically in Sicily) in July 1943. After a month-long battle, Operation Husky was successful, as territory was taken and the Germans retreated. The invasion of Italy could then begin.

When the Allied forces decided to open up a front in the West to complete the encirclement of Germany, Eisenhower was appointed to direct the Normandy landings (6 June 1944). He commanded the largest ever military invasion force, and managed to reconcile the temperaments of the different generals from France (Charles de Gaulle, 1890-1970), England (Bernard Montgomery Law, 1887-1976) and America (George Smith Patton, 1885-1945). The operation was a success, and led to the liberation of Europe from German domination.

Allied forces landing in Normandy on 6 June 1944.

POLITICAL CAREER

In 1948, Eisenhower opted to leave the army to become President of Columbia University, one of the most prestigious colleges in the country. Three years later, he left this post after his appointment as Supreme Commander of NATO, a position which confirmed his diplomatic skills. It was then that the Republican Party chose him as its candidate in the 1952 presidential election. He won the elections in a landslide and served as President of the United States from 1953 to 1961, having been reelected in 1956.

He retired from political life in 1961, after supporting the candidacy of his vice-president Richard Milhous Nixon (1913-1994). He then moved to Gettysburg, Pennsylvania, where he wrote his memoirs, while occasionally taking part in American political life. After falling ill, he died in a military hospital in Washington, D.C. on 28 March 1968.

POLITICAL, SOCIAL AND ECONOMIC CONTEXT

THE POSTWAR PERIOD AND THE START OF THE COLD WAR

When the Second World War ended with the victory of the Allied forces over totalitarian regimes, the world order was completely changed. Europe, which until that point had been dominant, was left worn out and ruined by five years of fighting which had destroyed a large proportion of its territory and infrastructure. This encouraged the emergence of two superpowers, namely the USA and the USSR. Although they had managed to get along in spite of their profound ideological differences during the war, relations between them quickly deteriorated, in particular during the conferences in Yalta and Potsdam (1945). During these talks, the victors had the daunting task of deciding how to divide up the world. The Western powers seized the opportunity to limit Russian influence in Europe by setting up elections in the countries formerly occupied by Germany. However, shortly after the conference, the Russians torpedoed the agreement by organising coups in Romania and Poland.

THE UNION OF SOVIET SOCIALIST REPUBLICS

The USSR (Union of Soviet Socialist Republics), which was created in 1922 by the Bolshevik Party, was a totalitarian state ruled with an iron fist by the Communist Party and men such as Lenin (1870-1924) and Joseph

Stalin (1878-1953). Along with China, it became the spearhead of the Communist International, which advocated a dictatorship of the proletariat, by nationalising national resources and the means of production and abolishing private property.

The USSR brought together 15 independent republics (Armenia, Azerbaijan, Belorussia, Estonia, Georgia, Kazakhstan, Kyrgyzstan, Latvia, Lithuania, Moldova, Russia, Tajikistan, Turkmenistan, Ukraine and Uzbekistan) in a federal republic, and remained the largest state in the world throughout the Cold War. It was dissolved on 26 December 1991, following declarations of independence by several countries.

Although the United Nations had been created in 1945 to ensure global security, tensions between the two blocs rose continuously and resulted in an ideological and political conflict known as the Cold War. Although the two superpowers only clashed militarily during the Korean War (1950-1953), the fear that a Third World War would break out was very real. Such a conflict would prove catastrophic for both sides due to the nuclear threat. The majority of the confrontations which occurred during this troubled period (such as the Vietnam War and the Soviet-Afghan War) took place without any direct clashes between the two armies. It was therefore more of a struggle for influence in non-aligned countries, where both sides tried to make their ideology prevail.

THE CONTAINMENT OF COMMUNISM AND THE RED SCARE

With the decline of colonial empires and the damage sustained during the Second World War, the baton of global leadership was passed to the United States. In the context of the Cold War, the approach of Eisenhower's predecessor Harry S. Truman (1884-1972) involved limiting the spread of Communism thanks to the Truman Doctrine, a policy of containment. According to Truman, the influence of the USSR should be contained within its borders through military and economic support provided to foreign countries which were fighting against the development of Communist states.

However, this fear of Communism, which was exacerbated by tensions between the countries, was also present within the USA, where the idea emerged that there were people in high places in the country who wanted to set up a totalitarian Communist regime there. This paranoia resulted in a virtual witch-hunt. In 1938, the House Un-American Activities Committee was set up to analyse activities that were deemed "un-American", and anyone accused before the Committee could lose their job and see their reputation tarnished. Its most vicious spokesperson, who managed to convince a large swathe of the public to subscribe to his ideas, was Senator Joseph McCarthy (1908-1957), after whom this repressive movement was named.

Photograph of Senator Joseph McCarthy.

From 1950 onwards, investigations were carried out with the aim of tracking Communist activists and sympathisers on American soil. This climate of violence reached its peak on 5 April 1951, when Julius Rosenberg (1918-1953) and his wife Ethel (1915-1953), engineers of Jewish origin, were sentenced to death for allegedly handing American scientific information over to the Communists. However, in the face of these methods, dissatisfaction began to emerge within the country, and in the mid-1950s McCarthy's popularity plummeted.

THE 1950S AND THE AFFLUENT SOCIETY

In spite of tensions in international politics, the American economy fared well in the 1950s and 1960s. The USA experienced a golden age which marked the high watermark of the American way of life. It was during this period that the concept of the Affluent Society developed.

Although economists feared that the end of the war economy would plunge the country into a major crisis due to the return of the soldiers and the end of the mass production of arms, the reality was completely different. Economic growth meant that the majority of Americans had jobs. The middle class grew and now enjoyed a high quality of life, compared with standards at the time.

Furthermore, by helping the European countries to rebuild themselves, the USA managed to double its agricultural and industrial production. It alone produced half the goods in the world. There was also a substantial population increase during this period as a result of the baby boom and medical advances, which reduced the mortality rate.

However, the lowest and most precarious social classes still did not benefit from this growth and prosperity. The gap between the richest and poorest members of society widened, in spite of the growth of the middle class, and 25% of the population lived below the poverty line. From then on, people in the cultural world spoke out against the American way of life and its inclination towards comfort and security, heralding the hippie movement of the 1960s.

RACIAL SEGREGATION AND CIVIL RIGHTS

Although the American Civil War (1861-1865) had put an end to slavery in the USA, African-Americans were still shut out of society. As such, in the early 1950s, there were still laws limiting their access to schools and public buildings in some Southern states, which remained opposed to the emancipation of black and Native American minorities. In spite of the efforts of the most progressive political groups, the situation moved forward thanks to movements of African-American citizens, who readily used the Supreme Court to improve their living conditions.

THE HIGHEST JUDICIAL AUTHORITY

The Supreme Court is the highest judicial authority in the United States. It comprises nine judges, one of whom presides over the Court, chosen from the most distinguished judges in the country. They are appointed for life and can only be dismissed by Congress.

The Court, which was established by Article III of the United States Constitution, most often rules on the revision of federal or state laws which are deemed unconstitutional. This is known as the power of judicial review. All the other courts in the country must respect

> its decisions and see that they are applied.

Thanks to Chief Justice Earl Warren (1891-1974), minorities secured major advances in terms of civil rights. The decisions taken during this period enabled the development of individual rights, such equal access to schools and equality before the law.

THE RACE FOR THE WHITE HOUSE IN 1952

After winning the Republican primaries, Eisenhower faced the Democratic candidate Adlai Stevenson. Stevenson was a well-known lawyer and provided a contrast to Eisenhower's simplicity: he was an intellectual and a regular guest of the greatest families in America. However, apart from these differences, the programmes presented by the two candidates were more or less the same, in terms of both domestic and foreign policy.

During the campaign, the conservatives' attacks focused on the Democrats' corruption and their failure to respond to the Communist threat. This was known as the K1C2 formula, which stands for "Korea, Communism and Corruption". The Republicans presented their candidate as a former war hero, a renowned diplomat and a respected figure, in stark contrast to the "socialist" Democrats who were tarnished by scandals and corrupted by their long years in power. In response, the Democrats were quick to attack Eisenhower's personality and highlight the divisions that had troubled the Republican Party throughout its history.

Eisenhower's presidential campaign, 1952.

This campaign was the first in which television had a clear influence on voters, in particular when the Republican vice-presidential candidate Richard Nixon, who was accused of having a slush fund for his campaign, delivered a speech which was later broadcast on television and watched by 60 million viewers. Whereas Eisenhower had previously asked his running mate to withdraw from the presidential race, his speech had such an impact that he changed his mind.

Eisenhower was elected with a 55% share of the vote, making him the first Republican president in 20 years. The Republican Party also held a majority in Congress (221 against 211 in the House of Representatives, and 48 against 47 in the Senate).

HIGHLIGHTS

A MODERATE PRESIDENT

Outside the normal political circles of the Republican Party, Eisenhower was elected above all for his aura as a victorious military general. The 4 November 1952 was therefore more the celebration of the triumph of a man than of a party.

He immediately formed a moderate government. He had the support of the business community and surrounded himself with people from the private sector who were experienced in administration. Like any good military man, he knew how to delegate some of his responsibilities to trusted collaborators and to avoid exposing himself directly to bad decisions. His cabinet was made up not of leaders of the Republican Party, but of men with hands-on experience, including the Secretary of Defense Charles Erwin Wilson (American engineer, 1890-1961), the former CEO of General Motors.

At the start of his presidency, Eisenhower's rhetoric was often aggressive and threatening, but his pragmatism soon led him towards prudence and diplomacy. He was a skilled negotiator, and generally tried to satisfy the different parties when making decisions. The first years of his presidency marked a major change compared with the Democratic administrations, but his critics noted above all that there was a significant discrepancy between his words and his actions.

PROGRESSIVE CONSERVATISM

After the misery of the Wall Street Crash of 1929, American presidents brought about major social advances, and Eisenhower was no exception to this rule. During his term, he extended social security and health insurance to seven million Americans and raised the minimum wage. At the same time, he implemented a policy of financing social housing from 1954 onwards. In spite of these advances, the gap between the richest and the poorest social classes remained large.

Shortly after his election, he defined his economic and social policy as "progressive conservatism". In terms of finance, there was state intervention in favour of businessmen, which led Truman to suggest that Eisenhower was a "stooge for Wall Street". He supported complete economic liberalism and advocated the least restrictive system of economic control possible, with the government only guaranteeing monetary stability. When he arrived in the White House, he removed price and wage controls, which had been in place since the war. However, because of the constantly rising unemployment rate, he could not limit state intervention as much as he had initially wanted to.

In a favourable economic context, he embarked on a series of large-scale state-financed projects: he organised the construction of a waterway connecting the Saint Lawrence River to the Great Lakes, and enacted the Federal Aid Highway Act of 1956, which provided $25 billion to build 41 000 miles of the Interstate Highway System. These projects enabled him to create millions of jobs, as the works were not completed until the mid-1990s. This project transformed and modernised the United States in the long term and improved internal connectivity, resulting in a boom in the automobile industry.

A CHANGE IN FOREIGN POLICY

Eisenhower managed to put an end to the Korean War, which had resulted in over a million deaths. This had been an important element of his platform during his campaign for the presidency. After the Korean Armistice Agreement was signed on 27 July 1953, the American government opted for a new strategy which involved using a strong dissuasive rhetoric in foreign policy, based in particular on nuclear intimidation, in order to limited the engagement of the armed forces in distant and protracted conflicts.

At the same time, his policy focused on creating a network of alliances with allied countries. Eisenhower therefore followed Truman's approach by continuing to provide financial and military support to developing countries, with the aim of securing their unconditional support against the Soviet Bloc.

If intervention could not be avoided, he wanted it to be as brief as possible. This was the case, for example, in Lebanon in 1958, when the US government intervened for three months at the request of the Lebanese government to fight a revolutionary movement that was seeking to topple the regime.

Secret operations were also carried out to defend American financial or ideological interests, as was the case in Guatemala in June 1954 and in Operation Ajax in Iran. The CIA became an important organisation because of its clear involvement in these regime changes.

A SECRET OPERATION IN IRAN

Operation Ajax was a secret operation carried out by the CIA in Iran. It aimed to put an end to the regime of the democratically elected Prime Minister Mohammad Mossadegh (1881-1967), who was nationalising the nation's oilfields. After a first failed attempt, CIA agents managed to make the people and soldiers close to the monarchy rise up thanks to staged attacks and demonstrations. The mission was a success and the monarchical power of the Shah (ruler in the Middle East) was restored through a coup d'état.

By intervening, the USA had wanted to protect the interests of the Anglo-Iranian Oil Company, a British corporation which had lost its control over the extraction of oil in the country. After the coup, the support of the new regime allowed the USA to distribute oil-drilling licences to American companies. The CIA's involvement was acknowledged by the American government in 2000, when Bill Clinton (born in 1946) was president.

However, the government chose not to intervene in every new fight against Communism. As such, when the Russian army violently repressed a national popular movement in Hungary that had managed to overthrow the existing Communist government, the USA did not come to its aid.

Likewise, during the Suez Crisis in 1956, the UN and the USA forced the British and French troops to withdraw from the canal they were occupying after it had been nationalised by the Egyptian president Gamal Abdel Nasser (1918-1970). Through this action, the USA distanced itself from these two allies which were concerned with protecting the interests of their colonial empires. Egypt was officially given control of the canal at the end of the year.

All these actions show the limits of the Eisenhower administration's talk of toughness and intimidation. Although there was certainly a rhetoric of reprisals and threats, this was adapted to the situation and the policy applied on the ground.

THE BEGINNINGS OF DESEGREGATION

During the 1950s, the movement towards desegregation was slow, which allowed the Southern states to maintain the status quo in terms of rights for racial minorities. This situation was made possible by the fact that Eisenhower was not fundamentally in agreement with the decisions on equal rights taken by the Supreme Court. Indeed, a few years later, he acknowledged that he had made a mistake in appointing Earl Warren Chief Justice of the Supreme Court: Eisenhower had thought that Warren was a traditionalist, but in reality he proved to be very progressive in his decisions.

However, the greatest advance in this area came in the landmark *Brown v. Board of Education* case. Linda Brown (born in 1942), an African-American student from Kansas, was refused access to a school because of racial segregation. With the support of the local chapter of the NAACP (National Association for the Advancement of Colored People), her family and others took the case to the Supreme Court. In May 1954, the Court ruled in their favour and compelled states to ensure equal access to schools, thus allowing black students to attend whites-only schools. In the years that followed, there were many demonstrations and incidents between supporters of segregation and governmental authorities in the South. It was only during his second term, in 1957, that Eisenhower sent federal forces to Little Rock (Arkansas), after the governor had closed a school that nine black children were due to attend. This presidential intervention accelerated the integration of schools in the Southern states of the USA.

Federal troops escort the "Little Rock Nine" into Little Rock Central High School.

In November 1956, after the African-American seamstress and activist Rosa Parks (1913-2005) refused to give up her seat on a bus for a white passenger, the Supreme Court ruled against segregation on public transport and struck down the law requiring black passengers to give up their seat for white passengers and to sit at the back of the bus. Finally, in 1957 there was a major step forward when Congress confirmed black citizens' right to vote, which was still not applied in some states.

THE END OF MCCARTHYISM

Eisenhower's first term also saw an end to the vicious intolerance of McCarthyism in 1954, when the Senate censured McCarthy and pushed him to the margins of political life.

Disowned by the president because of his repeated attacks on Eisenhower's former mentor General George Marshall, McCarthy saw his popularity plummet and the members of his own party turn against him as a result of his excesses and forcefulness during some questioning sessions. Although the fall of McCarthy did not put an end to the internal fight against Communism, it did mean that this fight was carried out less openly.

In spite of this, Eisenhower was convinced that the Rosenbergs were guilty and refused to pardon them. They were sent to the electric chair on 19 June 1953, despite international outcry. The Internal Security Act, which forced Communist organisations to register with the United States Attorney General with the aim of anticipating acts of sabotage, was amended by the government in 1954, so as to ban and bring to trial the activities of the American Communist Party, which was recognised as a subversive organisation.

REELECTION IN 1956 AND THE EISENHOWER DOCTRINE

Eisenhower was reelected in November 1956, winning 57% of the votes against Adlai Stevenson, who he had already beaten in 1952. This time he was left facing a Democratic majority in the House and Senate, but managed to govern with them without any serious problems, thanks to his capacities for mediation and moderation. Furthermore, following the end of McCarthyism and the Korean War, political tensions and internal divisions within the country were subsiding, allowing him to secure a broad consensus to govern.

After his reelection, he defined US foreign policy, focusing in particular on the Middle East with what became known as the Eisenhower Doctrine. Supported by Congress, this doctrine involved sending troops to help any country in the Middle East asking for support against aggression from a Communist country. The aim was to keep American influence intact in this important oil-producing region. The doctrine was applied when the USA intervened in Lebanon in 1958.

LESS TENSE RELATIONS WITH THE USSR

On 4 October 1957, the Cold War took a new turn when the USSR sent the first artificial satellite, Sputnik, into orbit. This sent shockwaves across the United States, which was stunned to be behind the USSR in the Space Race. In order to catch up, assistance funds were set up for national education. One year later, NASA was founded and was tasked with coordinating research in the aerospace and aeronautics fields.

The Secretary of State John Foster Dulles (1888-1959) then decided to develop a new policy, known as the New Look, with the aim of rolling back Communism through a dissuasive discourse involving the threat of massive reprisals, in particular through nuclear weapons. However, this discourse remained primarily theoretical and rhetorical. Finally, since Stalin's death in 1953, tensions between the two superpowers had subsided, and negotiations took place after Nikita Khrushchev (1894-1971) came to power in the same year. Three years later, Khrushchev developed the doctrine of peaceful coexistence between the two blocs.

Eisenhower and Khrushchev with their wives at a state dinner.

Soviet-American relations calmed down, in particular thanks to Khrushchev's visit to the USA in 1959. However, this new understanding was very fragile, and in 1960 an American U-2 reconnaissance aircraft was shot down by the Soviets over their territory. As Eisenhower did not provide any justification for this secret military incursion on Soviet territory, Khrushchev quit the 1960 Four Power Paris Summit, which was supposed to resolve the issue of the administration of Berlin. Relations between the two blocs would remain tense until Eisenhower's successor, John F. Kennedy (1917-1963) was elected.

THE FIRST OFFICIAL VISIT TO THE USA

The American tour undertaken by Khrushchev, the First Secretary of the Central Committee of the Communist Party, in September 1959 was the first official visit of a Communist leader to the USA since the start of the Cold War. This visit therefore symbolised the decline in tensions between the two great powers. Along with his family and some Soviet officials, Khrushchev visited a number of American cities before meeting Eisenhower at Camp David, the country retreat of the President of the United States, for two days. His aim was to find a solution to the problem of the enclave of West Berlin, situated in German Democratic Republic territory, by getting the Western powers to agree to withdraw their troops and turn it into a demilitarised zone. However, the rupture during the Four Powers Paris Summit led to the construction of the Berlin Wall in 1961.

IMPACT

THE VIETNAM WAR

While the French were fighting an independence movement supported by the Communist states during the First Indochina War (1946-1954), the USA decided to refrain from military intervention in the conflict, in spite of France's chaotic situation. They nonetheless agreed to grant the country financial aid. However, this was not enough, and in July 1954, the Geneva Accords put an end to the conflict after the surrender of the French troops.

The former French Indochina was then divided into two states: the Democratic Republic of Vietnam in the North, supported by the Communist nations, and the Republic of Vietnam in the South, supported by the USA and other Western countries. Although the Geneva Accords stated that a referendum on the reunification of the country was to be organised in 1956, Eisenhower's government, which anticipated and feared the victory of local Communist leaders if democratic elections were held, decided to ensure that this clause was not respected.

On the other hand, Eisenhower, who was wary of the spread of Communism in the region, promised to assist the South Vietnamese leaders and went as far as to send American advisors to the country to train the South Vietnamese army in February 1954. Following this major decision, the USA finally had to take over from France in the quagmire in Southeast Asia and provide constant support to the South

Vietnamese army against Communist movements.

In August, the situation worsened and the USA decided to intervene directly in order to push back Communist movements. However, the operation came to a standstill against an enemy which had a far better knowledge of the territory and which wore down the American troops through a campaign of guerrilla operations. The conflict ended in complete failure, and in 1975 the South was conquered by the North. The two countries were then unified and became the Socialist Republic of Vietnam, which was part of the Communist Bloc.

CUBA: A NEIGHBOUR AND AN ENEMY

The situation in Cuba also worsened at the end of the 1950s. After losing the support of the USA, the dictator Fulgencio Batista (1901-1973) was toppled by a revolutionary movement led by Fidel Castro (1926-2016).

Although Eisenhower's government initially recognised the new leader, this changed when he implemented Communist measures, for example by nationalising raw materials and removing the United Fruit Company, an American corporation. Eisenhower responded immediately by decreeing an embargo on certain key materials for the Cuban economy, such as sugar and petrol, in this way attempting to weaken the new regime. Castro's government reacted by aligning itself with the USSR and signing a series of economic and military aid agreements.

The situation did not improve, and in fact reached catastrophic proportions. The fiasco of the Bay of Pigs Invasion in 1961 drove the Cuban government to become an ally of the USSR, and Cuba became a Communist forward base, within firing range of the USA.

THE BAY OF PIGS INVASION

The Eisenhower administration was unhappy about the development of a Communist regime some 1500 miles from the American coast, and at the end of his term it decided to intervene in Cuba. As it could not attack the country directly, the CIA took around 1400 Cuban refugees from the USA so that they could topple Castro's regime.

After an aerial operation that destroyed a significant proportion of the Cuban air force, the combatants landed at a beach in the Bay of Pigs on 17 April 1961. Unable to count on the support of the local population, they were quickly stopped by the Cuban army and the operation was a complete failure.

One year later, the Cuban Missile Crisis, one of the results of this fiasco, almost descended into nuclear war when the Americans realised that the Russians were installing atomic missile launch facilities on the neighbouring island.

THE CIVIL RIGHTS MOVEMENT DURING THE 1960S

The process of racial desegregation begun in the 1950s reached its highest level of tension in the following decades, under the governments of John F. Kennedy and Lyndon B. Johnson (1908-1973). As he did not agree entirely with the movement's demands, Eisenhower delayed as much as possible the sweeping changes in this area, which were very challenging for the traditionalist society of the USA. Nonetheless, the limited advances of the 1960s resulted in a tense atmosphere in the following decade.

The Civil Rights Movement then carried out a range of actions to secure the necessary changes to the segregationist laws, such as sit-ins, which involved peacefully occupying a public place and refusing to move. At the March on Washington in 1963, which attracted between 200 000 and 300 000 participants, a leader emerged when the African-American pastor Martin Luther King, Jr. (1929-1968) delivered his famous "I Have a Dream" speech.

View from the Lincoln Memorial of the crowd gathered at the March on Washington.

Under increasing pressure from the public, there was a serious power struggle between the federal government and some of the country's Southern states (namely Alabama and North Carolina), which refused to apply the new constitutional changes. In this context, there were clashes in predominantly black ghettoes in some cities, resulting in a number of deaths.

Finally, the law changed with the Civil Rights Act of 1964, signed into law by President Johnson. This outlawed all forms of discrimination and abolished racial segregation in public buildings and administration. This was followed by the Voting Rights Act of 1965, which allowed black citizens to vote in some Southern states, where laws still limited their right to vote.

SUMMARY

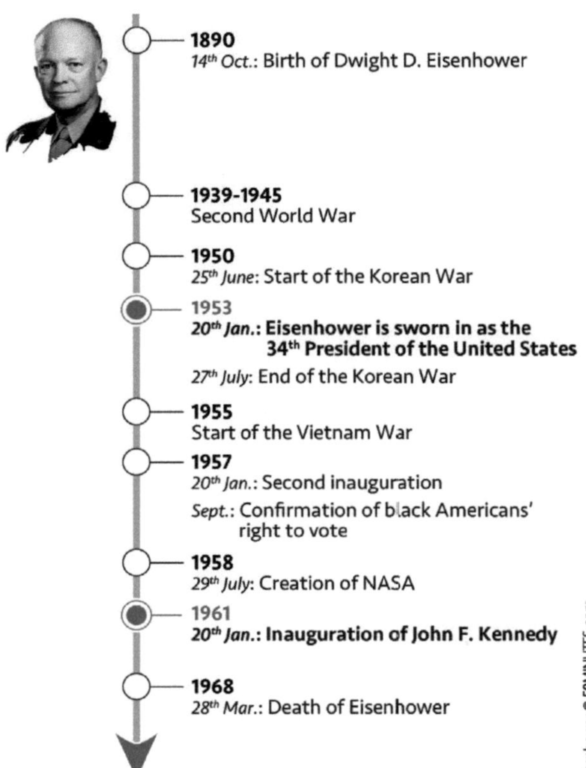

- Lauded as a hero after serving as Supreme Commander of the Allied Expeditionary Forces in Europe during the Normandy landings in the Second World War, Dwight David Eisenhower was elected in a landslide over his

Democratic rival in 1952 and 1956. He was a great diplomat and was admired by both Democrats and Republicans, and remains one of the most popular presidents of the 20th century.

- Although he wanted to liberalise the American economy as much as possible, he was never able to carry out all of his economic programme. However, he did improve transport connections within the USA through the creation of highways financed by the state. The Affluent Society also developed during his presidency, and the development of the American middle class gave rise to the so-called American way of life.
- The start of his presidency saw the end of McCarthyism, which ended when the Senate censured the man behind it. The period of internal tensions and witch-hunts was now over.
- In 1954, in spite of Eisenhower's apparent passivity with regard to advances in civil rights, the *Brown v. Board of Education* case before the Supreme Court made the first cracks in the system of racial segregation in the Southern states of the USA, which would collapse in the following decade.
- On 27 July 1953, Eisenhower put an end to the Korean War.
- In response to tensions in the Middle East, at the start of his second term he established the Eisenhower Doctrine in order to limit the influence of the Communist Bloc in this important oil-producing region.
- With the support of Nikita Khrushchev, the two blocs managed to peacefully coexist in spite of tensions caused by intermittent incidents. At the end of his presidency, a diplomatic issue prefigured the culmination of the

Cold War: the Vietnam War and the Cuban Missile Crisis, which would both unfold in the 1960s.

- In 1961, he decided to retire from political life after trying to warn the public of the growth of the military-industrial complex in the country and the rise of American militarism.
- He died on 28 March 1968.

We want to hear from you!
Leave a comment on your online library
and share your favourite books on social media!

FIND OUT MORE

BIBLIOGRAPHY

- Ambrose, S. (2003) *Eisenhower: Soldier and President.* London: Simon & Schuster.
- Eisenhower, D.D. (1963) *Mandate for Change, 1953-1956.* New York: Doubleday & Co.
- Eisenhower, D.D. (1965) *The White House Years: Waging Peace 1956-1961.* New York: Doubleday & Co.
- Fohlen, C. (1997) *De Truman à Eisenhower. Histoire des États-Unis.* Paris: Flammarion.
- Heffer, J. (1997) *Les États-Unis de 1945 à nos jours.* Paris: Armand Colin.
- Jacquard, R. (1998) *De Washington à Clinton. La galerie des presidents américains.* Paris: Jean Picollec.
- Kaspi, A. (2002) *Les Américains. Les États-Unis de 1945 à nos jours*, volume 2. Paris: Seuil.
- Kaspi, A. and Harter, H. (2013) *Les presidents américains. De Washington à Obama.* Paris: Tallandier.
- Lacroix, J.-M. (2013) *Histoire des États-Unis.* Paris: Presses universitaires de France.
- Mélandri, P. (2008) *Histoire des États-Unis contemporains.* Brussels: André Versaille.

ADDITIONAL SOURCES

- Alexander, C. (1975) *Holding the Line: The Eisenhower Era, 1952-1961.* Bloomington: Indiana University Press.
- Branyan, R.L. and Larsen, L. (1971) *The Eisenhower Administration, 1953-1961: A Documentary History.* New

York: Random House.

- D'Este, C. (2003) *Eisenhower: A Soldier's Life*. New York: Henry Holt and Company.
- Divine, R. (1981) *Eisenhower and the Cold War*. New York: Oxford University Press.
- Eisenhower, D.D. (1986) *Eisenhower: At War, 1943-1945*. New York: Random House.
- Gellman, I.F. (2017) *The President and the Apprentice: Eisenhower and Nixon, 1952-1961*. New Haven, Connecticut: Yale University Press.
- Halberstam, D. (1994) *The Fifties*. New York: Ballantine Books.
- Newton, J. (2012) *Eisenhower: The White House Years*. New York: Anchor Books.
- Pach, C. and Richardson, E. (1991) *The Presidency of Dwight D. Eisenhower*. Lawrence: University Press of Kansas.
- Smith, J.E. (2013) *Eisenhower in War and Peace*. New York: Random House.

ICONOGRAPHIC SOURCES

- Portrait of Dwight D. Eisenhower. Royalty-free reproduction picture.
- Allied forces landing in Normandy on 6 June 1944. Royalty-free reproduction picture.
- Photograph of Senator Joseph McCarthy. Royalty-free reproduction picture.
- Eisenhower's presidential campaign, 1952. Royalty-free reproduction picture.
- Federal troops escort the "Little Rock Nine" into Little

Rock Central High School. Royalty-free reproduction picture.
- Eisenhower and Khrushchev with their wives at a state dinner. Royalty-free reproduction picture.
- View from the Lincoln Memorial of the crowd gathered at the March on Washington. Royalty-free reproduction picture.

FILMS AND DOCUMENTARIES

- *Ike.* (1979) [Television mini-series]. Bob Sagal. Dir. USA: ABC Circle Films.
- *The Butler.* (2013) [Film]. Lee Daniels. Dir. USA: Follow Through Productions, Salamander Pictures, Laura Ziskin Productions, Lee Daniels Entertainment, Pam Williams Productions, Windy Hill Pictures.

50MINUTES.com
History
Business
Coaching
ISHIKAWA DIAGRAM
Anticipate and solve problems within your business
Material Method Machine
Mother Nature Measure Men
THE BATTLE OF AUSTERLITZ
NETWORKING